FICTION

Heather
Moore Niver

Enslow Publishing
101 W. 23rd Street
Suite 240
New York, NY 10011
USA

enslow.com

WORDS TO KNOW

author A person who writes.

character A person (or sometimes an animal) in a story, play, movie, or other work of literature.

graphic Having to do with art.

illustration A drawing.

imagination The act of making something in our mind.

literature Written work.

plot What happens in a story.

publish To make a book that will be sold.

setting One or more places where the action of a story happens.

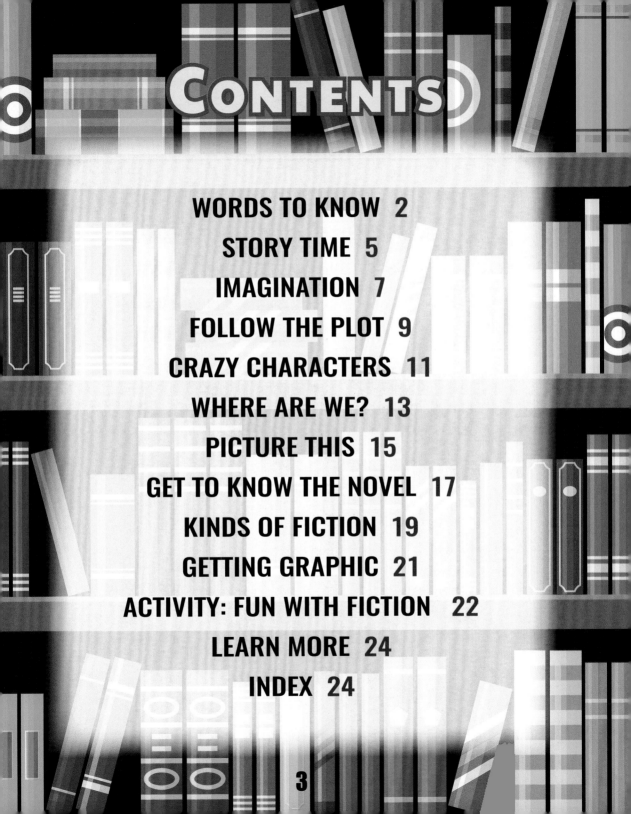

CONTENTS

Maurice Sendak wrote the popular children's book *Where the Wild Things Are.*

Story Time

What is your favorite story? Maybe you love *Green Eggs and Ham* by Dr. Seuss. Or *Where the Wild Things Are* by Maurice Sendak. These books are a kind of **literature** called fiction.

FAST FACT

Dr. Seuss was the first person to use the word "nerd." He used it in the 1950 story *If I Ran the Zoo.*

Shel Silverstein
wrote many
kinds of fiction.

Imagination

Fiction is a made-up story. Writers, called **authors**, make up stories. They use their **imagination** to write fiction. They make up the **characters** and the events in the story.

FAST FACT

Shel Silverstein is known for writing poems, plays, and songs, but he also wrote fun stories for kids. One of these was *Who Wants a Cheap Rhinoceros?*

In the plot of *Cinderella*, a girl is sent to a ball by her fairy godmother.

Follow the Plot

Every story needs an exciting **plot**. The plot is the series of events in the story. Movies, plays, and short stories all have plots.

Fern spends time with the animals in *Charlotte's Web*.

Crazy Characters

Characters are usually the people in the story. Sometimes characters are animals. In E. B. White's book *Charlotte's Web*, the main characters are Fern and the farm animals.

FAST FACT

E. B. White added the character of Fern to *Charlotte's Web* at the last minute.

The setting of *Winnie-the-Pooh* is the Hundred Acre Wood.

Where Are We?

The **setting** is the place where a story happens. It can be a town, a castle, or outer space. The time period is also part of the setting, like a story that takes place during the Civil War.

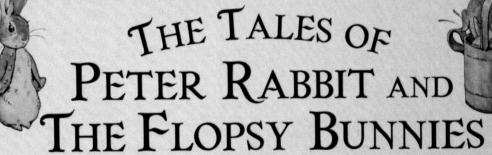

The Tales of
Peter Rabbit and
The Flopsy Bunnies

THE ORIGINAL AND AUTHORIZED EDITIONS BY
BEATRIX POTTER
F. WARNE & CO.

TM

**Beatrix Potter
wrote some of the
first picture books.**

Picture This

Picture books are a popular form of fiction for young people. They tell a story with lots of **illustrations**. The pictures in these books are just as important as the words!

Fast Fact

Every year, the Caldecott Medal is awarded to an outstanding American picture book.

Roald Dahl

Charlie and the Great Glass Elevator

THE WORLD'S
★ No.1 ★
STORYTELLER

Roald Dahl wrote
many popular novels
for young people.

illustrated by Quentin Blake

Get to Know the Novel

Novels are a long form of fiction. Novels often tell a long story with lots of details. They are divided into chapters. The story may also have lots of different characters.

FAST FACT

A short novel is called a novella.

Edgar Allan Poe was a famous mystery writer.

Kinds of Fiction

Fiction comes in many styles. Romances tell love stories. In mysteries, characters try to solve a kind of puzzle. Science fiction tells a story based on science facts or technology.

FAST FACT

Edgar Allan Poe is famous for writing the first detective story, "The Murders in the Rue Morgue," in 1841.

Lincoln Peirce
writes the Big Nate
graphic novels.

Getting Graphic

Another type of fiction is the **graphic** novel. They look like comic strips in book form. Graphic novels mix words and pictures to tell a story.

FAST FACT

The first graphic novel was **published** in 1978.

Activity

Fun with Fiction

Want to write your own fiction? Here is

MATERIALS
books
paper
pencils

how to get started:

Grab two or three of

your favorite books.

What do you like

about them? Where is the beginning, middle, and end of each story?

Now think of a story you'd like to tell. Start by drawing pictures of the different parts of the tale. You can also cut out pictures from magazines or even take your own photos and print them out. Put the pictures in order. You have made a storyboard!

Now start to write your story by telling what is happening in each picture. Start with at least one sentence for each picture.

Learn More

Books

Holub, Joan. *Little Red Writing*. San Francisco, CA: Chronicle Books, 2016.

Lynette, Rachel. *Frank and Fiona Build a Fictional Story*. Chicago, IL: Norwood House Press, 2014.

Roza, Greg. *What Is Fiction?* New York, NY: Britannica Educational Publishing, 2015.

Websites

Making Books for Families
www.makingbooks.com / families. shtml#books
Check out these fun ideas for making your own books to tell your stories, either by yourself or with an adult's help.

Story Starters
www.thestorystarter.com / jr.htm
Need an idea for a story? Check out this award-winning website for thousands of ideas!

Index

Published in 2019 by Enslow Publishing, LLC.
101 W. 23rd Street, Suite 240, New York, NY 10011

Copyright © 2019 by Enslow Publishing, LLC.

All rights reserved.

No part of this book may be reproduced by any means without the written permission of the publisher.

Library of Congress Cataloging-in-Publication Data

Names: Niver, Heather Moore, author.
Title: Fiction / Heather Moore Niver.
Description: New York, NY : Enslow Publishing, LLC., [2019] | Series: Let's learn about literature | Audience: K-4 |Includes bibliographical references and index.
Identifiers: LCCN 2017045159| ISBN 9780766095984 (library bound) | ISBN 9780766096004 (pbk.) | ISBN 9780766096011 (6 pack)
Subjects: LCSH: Fiction genres—Study and teaching (Elementary) | Literary form—Study and teaching (Elementary) | Language arts (Elementary)
Classification: LCC PN3427 .N58 2017 | DDC 808.3—dc23
LC record available at https://lccn.loc.gov/2017045159

Printed in the United States of America

To Our Readers: We have done our best to make sure all website addresses in this book were active and appropriate when we went to press. However, the author and the publisher have no control over and assume no liability for the material available on those websites or on any websites they may link to. Any comments or suggestions can be sent by email to customerservice@enslow.com.

Photo Credits: Cover, p. 1 Africa Studio/Shutterstock.com; pp. 2-3, 24 Gurza/Shutterstock.com; p. 4 James Keyser/The LIFE Images Collection/Getty Images; pp. 5, 7, 9, 11, 13, 15, 17, 19, 21, 22-23 (paper, notebook, pencil) narmacero/Shutterstock.com; pp. 5, 7, 11, 15, 17, 19, 21, 22 (open book) Wen Wen/Shutterstock.com; p. 6 Alice Ochs/Michael Ochs Archives/Getty Images; p. 8 Buyenlarge/Archive Photos/Getty Images; p. 10 United Archives GmbH/Alamy Stock Photo; p. 12 CBW/Alamy Stock Photo; p. 14 Carolyn Jenkins/Alamy Stock Photo; p. 16 The Advertising Archives / Alamy Stock Photo; p. 18 Rischgitz/Hulton Archive/Getty Images; p. 20 Portland Press Herald/Getty Images; p. 22 ESB Professional/Shutterstock.com.